I0706770

MAGNIFICENT MAXI

A Happy Child Successfully Swinging the Swings of Bipolar Disorder

Barbara Arner

CHAPTER 1

There once was a child named Maxi and her dog Darcy. They loved each other. One morning they both woke up.

Maxi said to Darcy, "I am feeling very sad."

Darcy replied, "What's wrong?"

Maxi began to cry and said to Darcy, "I don't know. I am just sad. I don't feel well. I have a stomachache and headache and my body hurts." She continued to cry. Darcy was so confused as to why Maxi was so sad. Nothing bad happened; she just woke up very, very sad.

Darcy said to Maxi, "Why don't we get out of bed and have breakfast?"

Maxi slowly got out of bed and followed Darcy downstairs. She slowly fed Darcy her breakfast and slowly poured herself a bowl of cereal. Maxi ate only a couple spoonfuls of cereal and then stopped.

"I'm not hungry, Darcy," she said and began to cry again.

Darcy replied to Maxi, "How about we go outside for a walk in the sun? Maybe that will make you feel better."

Maxi slowly put on Darcy's leash and they went outside. Maxi did not want to play or walk. She walked just a couple of steps. Then she started to cry again.

Darcy did not know why her beloved owner was feeling so sad and crying so much. Darcy wanted Maxi to feel better and to be happy. Darcy began to run around trying to play with Maxi excitedly wagging her tail and licking her. But Maxi just stood there and continued to cry and was so very sad.

Maxi and Darcy went back inside and went upstairs and crawled back into bed and snuggled. Darcy was so sad Maxi was not feeling well. Maxi did not want to see anyone or talk to anyone. She wanted to be alone; only with Darcy. Darcy was very comforting to her. Maxi felt safe and secure as she held Darcy close to her.

Darcy said to Maxi, "I will always love you no matter how sad you feel. I will always be here for you. I am never leaving."

Maxi began to cry again and Darcy licked away her tears and they drifted off to sleep.

COLORING ACTIVITY

Create a safe place.

Maxi's safe and comfortable place is being with Darcy. She feels better when she pets her and they snuggle. Draw a picture of a person, place, or thing that makes you feel comfortable, safe, and secure when you are feeling sad.

*For the caregiver: This art therapy directive will enable you to provide this safe haven when your child is feeling depressed and needs to be comforted.

CHAPTER 2

After sleeping in bed sad and tired for a couple hours, Darcy licked Maxi and she began to wake up. Maxi hugged Darcy and was feeling better. No longer crying.

Darcy asked Maxi, "Do you want to get up and have lunch and then go to the playground?"

Maxi got out of bed and they went downstairs to have lunch. Maxi started to laugh and was being silly. She didn't want to eat and quickly told Darcy she wanted to go to the playground now. Maxi ran to get Darcy's leash in a hurry and quickly put it on her. She moved very fast. She ran Darcy up the street to the playground. Darcy was exhausted and breathing heavy, but Maxi just ran and ran. She began to play quickly on everything – up and down the slide and up and down, ran to the swing set and swung higher and higher jumping off. Maxi continued to run and laugh to herself giddily and silly with excitement. She was talking very loud and fast. Darcy did not know where she got all this energy from. A few hours ago she was so sad and crying for no reason and now she was laughing and running around talking so fast to herself. Darcy just laid down still exhausted from the run to the playground.

Then Maxi screamed out, "I can fly! I have magical superpowers! I can fly!"

Darcy was so confused as to why she was acting this way and thinking these thoughts that were not true. Maxi continued to swing and jump and run and talk loudly and laugh to herself. Darcy was so confused as she watched Maxi with her high energy. She kept running everywhere at the playground by herself and didn't even stop once to take a break or a breath. Darcy just didn't understand why she was acting this way. It did not look right to Darcy. Darcy asked Maxi if she wanted to sit and rest on the bench.

But she responded, "No! I have superpowers! I am flying!"

She continued to run around the slide, the swing set, the benches, anything and everything she could. Continuously laughing. Darcy asked Maxi to sit but she wouldn't. "Where did Maxi get all this energy from?" wondered Darcy. Maxi kept laughing to herself, running around, and being silly. Darcy was so confused. She was doing this all by herself as if she were in her own world. She wasn't playing or talking to the other children – just running, screaming, and laughing to herself, all by herself. She began to dangerously jump off the swing thinking she could fly. Darcy was so worried and concerned that she would hurt herself. Darcy kept trying to talk to Maxi, but Maxi just continued on and on. Finally, Darcy intervened running after her and barking loudly. Maxi fell to the ground and began laughing. Then Maxi started to cry and cry. Darcy was so worried and confused. She was sad this morning, had lots of energy this afternoon, and now sad again.

Darcy brought her leash to Maxi, but she was too upset to be able to put it on. Darcy just held it in her mouth and began to lead Maxi home. Maxi was too confused to know where to go. She kept crying and then laughing and then crying again. Darcy knew that something was very wrong. Maxi has never acted this way before. Darcy was getting so worried Maxi was not being her usual happy self. She was crying so much that she didn't know the way home and just followed Darcy. Maxi was so confused and upset and was not thinking properly. She started to laugh and cry again at the same time. She followed Darcy home and Darcy nudged the door open for her. Maxi started to get so very upset and was becoming angry now. Darcy just watched her scared and did not know what to do. Darcy loved her owner and cared very deeply about her and wanted her to be okay. Darcy wanted to see Maxi happy again. Then Maxi began to scream and scream in anger and rage and frustration. She had no control over her emotions. She cried and cried and cried and continued to scream. She didn't understand what was going on. Everything felt so scary and out of her control.

She ran up to her bedroom and was so very sad. She ran to her bed and began to sob and sob into her pillow. She did not understand what was happening to her. She had never felt this way before. Her emotions were so strong and she could not think clearly. She did not understand why she was talking so fast and running around and laughing to herself, then crying and screaming now.

Darcy was so concerned about what just happened. Darcy slowly walked up the stairs to Maxi's bedroom to see her. She was red hot and breathing heavy and continued to cry into her pillow. Darcy slowly walked up to Maxi and gave her kisses on her hand. Her crying slowed down a little. Then Darcy jumped on the bed and laid down next to her. Maxi petted her and began to calm down. She hugged Darcy and Darcy licked away her tears. Maxi tightly held on to Darcy. She was exhausted and scared and was trembling.

COLORING ACTIVITY

Think about how your body feels when you are angry. Using colors, lines, shapes, and images draw a picture of what your body and anger looks like. Give your drawing a title.

*For the caregiver: Many children have difficulty verbalizing their feelings. This art therapy directive will give your child an outlet to safely express themselves and their anger visually. This will better enable you to see how they are feeling internally. Encourage your child to explain their drawing to you.

COLORING ACTIVITY

Draw a picture of a quiet activity you can do to calm down when you feel angry or have too much excited energy.

*For the caregiver: This art therapy directive will reveal to you an activity you can safely provide for your child when they have too much manic energy.

CHAPTER 3

Darcy was so worried about Maxi. Maxi was so upset and Darcy had never seen her like this before. Maxi was still shaking and crying.

"How can I help?" Darcy asked Maxi.

"I don't know," Maxi replied.

Darcy continued, "When I am not feeling well, you take me to the vet to find out what is wrong with me and then I feel better. Maybe someone will make you feel better, too."

Maxi did not know what to do and was still very upset, shaking, and scared.

Darcy went downstairs and picked up the phone like Maxi does when Darcy is not feeling well. The only number Darcy saw on the phone was "911" written in red. Darcy dialed this number and someone immediately answered.

"911," the person responded.

"Hi. My name is Darcy. My owner Maxi is not feeling well. She keeps crying and crying and is very, very sad. She was also laughing so much and saying she had superpowers and could fly. I'm very worried about her," Darcy told her.

"She should see a doctor as soon as possible. He will make her feel better," the nice person said.

Darcy thought this was a very good idea to get help by seeing a doctor.

The kind person on the phone said to Darcy, "There is a doctor down the street that you can walk to. He is in a white cottage."

"That sounds like a very good idea to see a doctor. Thank you for helping," Darcy replied and then said good-bye.

Darcy went upstairs to her very sad owner.

"I called 911 and the person that answered said you should see a doctor now so you will feel better," Darcy calmly said to Maxi.

"I think that is a very good idea to get help," Maxi said to Darcy.

"The doctor is down the street in a white cottage and we can walk there together," Darcy said.

Maxi got out of bed and followed Darcy downstairs. They walked out together and went down the street looking for the white cottage.

Darcy and Maxi saw the white cottage. There were acres and acres of green grass, colorful flowers around the cottage, some in beautiful planters, and the sun was shining with a bright blue sky today. They walked in together.

There were chairs and tables with magazines in the room. There was also a tall, potted green tree in the corner.

Maxi sat down in one of the chairs and Darcy sat on the floor by her side.

Within less than a minute, a man walked out wearing a light pink shirt and tan pants. He said "hi" to Maxi and Darcy in a very soft voice and kindly smiled. He seemed very nice.

He invited Maxi and Darcy into his office and closed the door behind them. There was a huge brown desk with many papers on it and a big black leather swivel chair behind it. There were two blue chairs across from the desk. He sat down in the big black chair behind the desk and welcomed her to sit in a blue chair.

Maxi sat down in the blue chair. It was soft and she sank right down into it. It was very comfy. Darcy sat at her feet. Maxi suddenly felt calm in his office. It was so different than what she felt like the entire day. She now felt comfortable, safe, and secure. The doctor smiled and was very nice. He had a Snoopy phone on his desk which made her laugh. This doctor liked to talk. A lot. He made her feel very comfortable with his soft voice and kindness.

Finally, the doctor said to Maxi, "How was your day?"

Maxi did not know what to say, so Darcy started to talk to the doctor for her.

"Maxi woke up very sad and was crying," Darcy began. "Then we went to the playground and she was very excited and laughing and running around by herself. She thought she had superpowers and could fly and kept jumping off the swing. I got very scared she would hurt herself so I walked her back home. She was confused and did not know the way home.

When we returned, she started to cry and scream and then went into her bed and was scared and shaking. I called 911 and they told me I should bring her to see you."

The doctor closely listened to every word Darcy had to say and did not interrupt. When Darcy finished, the doctor happily smiled and said to them, "I am very glad you came to see me. You will feel better soon."

Maxi was so happy to hear that. He was such a nice doctor!

He continued, "I am a psychiatrist. I help people who have mental illnesses. A mental illness is a disorder of the brain that does not make you feel well. These disorders change your mood, thinking, and behavior. I can help you to feel better."

This psychiatrist was already making Maxi feel better. Maxi and Darcy listened closely to every word he had to say.

"There is medicine I can give you to help make you feel better," he explained.

Maxi was so happy to hear that. She didn't want to feel as awful as she did today. Darcy smiled too and was happy.

The psychiatrist said to Maxi, "You have a mood disorder called 'bipolar disorder.' Bipolar disorder is a brain disorder that causes episodes with changes in mood, energy, and activity level. Sometimes bipolar disorder makes you feel like you have a lot of energy and feel very excited like when you did when you were running around on the playground by yourself. You may not be able to stop laughing at something that no one else thinks is funny or be mad at something that doesn't make anyone else mad. You may get very angry or irritable. You can also have many thoughts in your head at one time, and these thoughts may come very quickly. You may not be able to keep your mind on what you are doing or not be able to sit still. You may also not want to sleep very much and you may want to stay up all night doing things. You may talk faster and louder than everyone else and get mad if someone stops you. This is the high, excited bipolar mood state called 'mania.'

You could also do dangerous things. You may think you have special powers which are not true like when you thought that you could fly off the swing at the playground. You could also hear voices telling you to do something, or see people or things that are not really there. These untrue thoughts are called 'psychosis.'"

The psychiatrist continued, "On the low, opposite side of bipolar disorder is depression. That is how you felt this morning when you woke up. Depression is feeling very sad. When you are depressed you might not enjoy anything – even things that used to be fun. You may cry a lot. You may feel angry. You may also feel lonely like no one cares about you. You may also get upset easily. You may not be able to sleep, or you may sleep too much. You may not want to eat, or you may want to eat all the time. You may have a hard time paying attention. Your body may also feel heavy like you can't move or talk. You may not feel like seeing friends or talking on the phone. You may also have a headache or stomachache. You could also think about hurting yourself. If you have thoughts of hurting yourself, you should tell someone you feel comfortable talking to and see a psychiatrist. If you don't have anyone to talk to, you should call 911. They will be nice and help you. These bad feelings will pass and you will feel better again."

The psychiatrist continued to talk to Maxi.

"What do you like to do, Maxi?" he asked.

"I like to make art, especially pottery. I like to go to the beach and swim. In the winter, I like to ski. And, of course, always being with Darcy. We like to go for walks, play fetch, and go to the playground," Maxi said.

The psychiatrist listened to Maxi very closely and smiled.

"You should go back home and do some pottery and go to the beach and swim," he said.

Maxi loved that idea and was so happy.

The psychiatrist also said to Maxi that she should also take Darcy for a walk and play with her. Darcy wagged her tail and smiled – she was excited about that idea!

This psychiatrist was such a nice person. He made Maxi happy. He was so kind and they laughed a lot. Darcy was very comfortable and happy, too.

The psychiatrist continued, "Would you like to come back to see me again next week?"

Maxi responded, "Yes, I would like to."

She had so much fun talking to him. This psychiatrist made Maxi laugh and definitely cheered her up. She felt so much better. She was calm, relaxed, and felt much different than when she arrived.

"I will give you some medicine to take and I will see you next week on the same day and time," he said to Maxi.

That sounded very simple to Maxi. Darcy was happy too, wagging her tail. The psychiatrist petted Darcy and he warmly smiled at them and said to enjoy the rest of their day. Then he said "bye" in the gentlest way.

Maxi said "thank you" to this very kind psychiatrist. She felt like he miraculously saved her and made her feel happy again.

COLORING ACTIVITY

Draw a picture of something you like to do that cheers you up when you are feeling sad.

*For the caregiver: This art therapy directive will reveal to you an activity you can offer to your child to help them feel better when they are depressed.

CHAPTER 4

A week went by and Maxi felt so much better. She was happy now and Darcy was so glad she was feeling better, too.

Maxi and Darcy walked back to the psychiatrist's white cottage.

He walked out of his office and kindly smiled and softly said "hi" to Maxi and Darcy. He invited them back into his office. It felt so good to see him and be there again. Maxi, once again, sank into the comfy blue chair and Darcy sat at her feet. Maxi and Darcy were very happy to be there again. The psychiatrist was happy to see them again as well. Maxi, Darcy, and the psychiatrist talked and laughed a lot. Maxi cried a little because she was sad about what happened to her but he made her feel better about it. The psychiatrist and she talked about her week – what she did and how she was feeling. Maxi told him she and Darcy were so much happier and she even took Darcy swimming in the ocean. The psychiatrist listened closely to every word Maxi said. He made her feel so much better about herself. He told her to do more of what made her happy. Maxi thought that sounded like a wonderful idea! She started telling him all these ideas and dreams she had for when she grows up. She felt so hopeful about her future. He told her she could be anything she wanted to be. She thought that was the nicest thing anyone had ever said to her. It was like he believed in her.

Maxi left the psychiatrist's office now feeling very, very good about herself and her life. Darcy was very happy for her, too. As always, she said "thank you" to this kind psychiatrist. The psychiatrist and Maxi smiled at each other and they softly said "bye" and she walked out.

COLORING ACTIVITY

Draw a picture of something you like to do that makes you feel happy.

*For the caregiver: This art therapy directive will reveal to you an activity your child can engage in to enhance the positive feelings of happiness in themself and with their life.

CHAPTER 5

On the walk back home, Darcy said to Maxi, "I am so happy you are feeling better. I was very worried and sad you were so unhappy. You are so strong and brave for going through what you did. I am so proud of you. It is so important you are taking care of yourself by seeing the psychiatrist and taking your medicine. I will be here for you always and forever."

Maxi truly felt strong and brave for going through and surviving her bipolar disorder episode. She was proud of herself and thankful she had Darcy who loved her and who helped take care of her when she couldn't take care of herself. Darcy kept her safe. And she was so thankful to this psychiatrist for always taking such good care of her and making her happy and laugh every time she saw him. Her life was much better now and she felt hopeful about her future.

COLORING ACTIVITY

Make a list of your strengths. These can describe how you feel about yourself and having bipolar disorder. Maxi felt "strong," "brave," and "hopeful."

*For the caregiver: This art therapy directive will give your child an opportunity to think about themselves and their success of surviving bipolar disorder in a positive light which will, consequently, enhance their self-esteem and self-worth.

CHAPTER 6

"Wow!" Maxi thought. "This was all so amazing. I am doing things I love, feeling good about myself, feeling okay about having bipolar disorder, and enjoying my life again."

Maxi said to Darcy, "Thank you for being so very nice to me and for loving me. Thank you for calling for help and taking me to the psychiatrist. You both saved my life. Thank you so much. I love you."

Darcy replied, "I love you too, Maxi. I will always be here for you forever and ever."

Maxi wanted Darcy to be happy too, of course. Darcy had been so loving to her and took such good care of her when she couldn't take care of herself.

Maxi put on Darcy's leash, grabbed some dog treats and a ball, and they happily walked down to the playground together. They played fetch and Darcy and she were so happy to be with each other having fun again. Darcy ran around with the other dogs, and Maxi played with the other children. Maxi thought of her psychiatrist and was grateful she had him in her life to help her live a happy, healthy, productive, and fun life while having bipolar disorder. She was very lucky. And now everyone was happy.

COLORING ACTIVITY

How are you feeling now? Draw a large circle below, and then using colors, lines, shapes, and images draw a picture inside the circle to express this feeling. Give your drawing a title.

*For the caregiver: This art therapy directive will give you a concrete idea of your child's current state of mind of how they are feeling: manic, depressed, or stable. Encourage your child to explain their drawing and feelings to you.

COLORING ACTIVITY

Lastly, draw a picture of yourself. Give your drawing a title.

*For the caregiver: This art therapy directive will give you an opportunity to observe how your child sees themself. It will give you information to share with their psychiatrist and therapist to aid in the therapeutic process of personal healing and growth which will enable them to lead a happy, healthy, and successful life while managing their bipolar disorder.